Sons of the American Revolution

History, constitution, by-laws, membership

Sons of the American Revolution

History, constitution, by-laws, membership

ISBN/EAN: 9783337202934

Printed in Europe, USA, Canada, Australia, Japan

Cover: Foto ©Andreas Hilbeck / pixelio.de

More available books at **www.hansebooks.com**

CALIFORNIA SOCIETY

OF THE

Sons of the American Revolution

Instituted at SAN FRANCISCO October 22nd, 1875

LIBERTAS ET PATRIA

1897

History

Constitution and By=Laws

Membership

California Society

OF THE

Sons of the American Revolution

Instituted at SAN FRANCISCO October 22nd, 1875

AS

SONS OF REVOLUTIONARY SIRES

"The first body in inception, institution and organization, to unite the descendants of Revolutionary patriots and perpetuate the memory of all those who took part in the American Revolution and maintained the Independence of the United States of America."

Constitution Adopted August 7, 1876.

Change of Name to Sons of the American Revolution, March 22, 1890.

New Constitution in Conformity to National Society S. A R., adopted October 19, 1891.

Constitution Amended October 19, 1896.

Society of the
Sons of the American Revolution.

INSTITUTED OCTOBER 22, 1875
SAN FRANCISCO, CAL.

Presidents:

DR. PETER WILKINS RANDLE, died, San Francisco, January 13, 1884.

GENERAL ALBERT M. WINN, died, Sonoma, Cal., August 26, 1883,
>   *(Made President-General at Third National Congress,*
>   *April 30, 1892.)*

HON. CALEB T. FAY, died, San Francisco, April 20, 1885.

CAPTAIN AUGUSTUS C. TAYLOR, son of a Revolutionary soldier, died,
San Francisco, September 3, 1891.

MR. LORING PICKERING, died, San Francisco, December 28, 1892.

COLONEL A. S. HUBBARD, San Francisco, California,
>   *(Made President-General at First National Congress,*
>   *April 30, 1890.)*

Organized as a NATIONAL SOCIETY in New York City, April 30, May 1 and 2, 1889.

Presidents General:

HON. LUCIUS P. DEMING, New Haven, Conn.; elected by the Organizing
Convention; resigned November 23, 1889.

DR. WILLIAM SEWARD WEBB, Shelburn, Vermont; elected for unexpired
term November 23, 1889; re-elected at First National Congress,
Louisville, Ky., April 30, 1890; again re-elected at Second
National Congress, Hartford, Conn., April 30, 1891.

GENERAL HORACE PORTER, New York City; elected at Third National
Congress, New York City, April 30, 1892; re-elected at the First
Triennial Conclave, Chicago, Ill., June 16, 1893, and for the third
time at Fifth National Congress, Washington, D. C., April 30,
1894, and for the fourth time at Sixth National Congress, Boston,
May 14, 1895, and for the fifth time at Seventh National Congress,
Richmond, Va., April 30, 1896.

HON. EDWIN SHEPARD BARRETT, Concord, Mass.; Eighth National
Congress, Cleveland, Ohio, April 30, 1897.

Provisional President.

———

Dr. Peter Wilkins Randle,
October 22, 1875, to July 4, 1876.

———

Presidents.

———

General Albert M. Winn,
July 4, 1876, to October 19, 1881.

Hon. Caleb T. Fay,
October 19, 1881, to July 5, 1882.

Captain Augustus C. Taylor,
July 5, 1882, to July 9, 1884.

Mr. Loring Pickering,
July 9, 1884, to July 5, 1886.

Colonel A. S. Hubbard,
July 5, 1886, to February 22, 1892.

John W. Moore, U. S. N.,
February 22, 1892, to February 22, 1893.

Captain J. Estcourt Sawyer, U. S. A.,
February 22, 1893, to February 22, 1894.

Charles J. King,
February 22, 1894, to February 22, 1895.

Lieutenant-Colonel Edward Hunter, U. S. A.,
February 22, 1895, to February 22, 1896.

Hon. Elisha W. McKinstry,
February 22, 1896, to January 12, 1897.

Mr. Sidney Mason Smith,
January 12, 1897.

Life Members.

GENERAL ULYSSES S. GRANT,
Died June 23, 1885.

HENRY McLEAN MARTIN,
Died April 5, 1891.

Honorary Members.

HON. HAMILTON FISH,
Died September 7, 1893.

GENERAL RUTHERFORD B. HAYES,
Died January 17, 1893.

BENSON J. LOSSING, LL.D.,
Died June 4, 1891.

GENERAL ALEX. S. WEBB, U. S. A.

LUCIUS P. DEMING, LL.D.

MAJOR GEORGE B. HALSTEAD, U. S. Vol.

LIEUTENANT JAMES C. CRESAP, U. S. N.

GENERAL BENJAMIN HARRISON.

HON. GROVER CLEVELAND.

MAJOR WM. McKINLEY.

Historical.

COLONEL RICH'D H. SAVAGE, Chief Aid to GEN'L JOHN McCOMB, the Grand Marshal chosen by the citizens of the City and County of San Francisco to provide and in a fitting manner arrange for the celebration of the Anniversary of American Independence, in his address, dated June 17th, 1875, to the people invoking their aid and co-operation, said:

"The near approach of the Ninety-ninth Anniversary of the Declaration of American Independence is the signal to invoke good citizens to aid in perfecting the arrangements for a fitting celebration of the honored day.

* * * * * * * * *

"Without partisan or sectional bias, looking only to the glorious national memories of the past and to the prosperous future stretching far before us, let us, dwellers by the Western Sea, send back a loyal greeting to our fellow-citizens nearer the birthplace of National Freedom.

"The first century of American freedom draws to its glorious close. National trials and struggles for existence have not shattered the noble fabric of Republican self-government, cemented as it is by the blood of our Revolutionary forefathers. Looking backward to the early vicissitudes of our National existence, the American citizen sees in the high-souled patriotism of the Revolution the grandest model of duty and self-devotion. Let us fittingly honor the day, the men, the deed. The Independence of America! its proclamation gave hope to suffering millions; its achievement has given happiness to a vast nation, in wealth and numbers far surpassing the most sanguine hopes of the many heroes who fought for posterity, who died that we might be free. In peaceful enjoyment of the freedom so dearly purchased, let us, as a grateful body of fellow-citizens, forget any dividing line in the one proud boast that we are Americans."

One of the results of Col. Savage's appeal was the formation and appearance in the procession of a platoon of soldiers in Continental dress, commanded by Capt. F. C. M. Fenn, who subsequently became a member of the California Society of the Sons of Revolutionary Sires.

The *Daily Alta* of July 6th, 1875, said of Capt. Fenn's command: "It was a marked feature of the procession, and as they marched past in their antique uniform, one almost fancied that the procession was a pageant of the 17th century, rather than a celebration of this age of military and civic enlightenment." And further says: "The names of celebrated battlefields and heroes of the Revolution, the separate letters of the words entwined in evergreen wreaths, the whole suspended across the streets, were handsome and were generally admired."

The call issued by Col. Savage took root in fertile soil, for at about this period a few patriotic and enthusiastic citizens of San Francisco, descendants of the early emigrants and colonists of America, were quietly moving and endeavoring to bring to the notice of their immediate associates of American blood and birth the duty of honoring the founders of the American nation, and of perpetuating the principles for which these heroes "pledged their lives and their sacred honor," and of producing a higher appreciation of the responsibilities and obligations of American citizenship.

Scarcely had the echoes of the celebration of Independence Day died away, when the sentiments aroused on that occasion assumed form and expression. A hundred days later, Friday evening, October 22nd, 1875, a meeting of descendants of soldiers, sailors and patriots of the Revolutionary War was called at the office of Dr. James L. Cogswell, No. 230 Kearny street, San Francisco. Among those present at this meeting were Major Edwin A. Sherman, Deputy U. S. Surveyor-General for Nevada, Ira C. Root, Dr. P. W. Randle, Rush R. Randle, Joseph Weed, Dr. Emory L. Willard and others, "who, when convened, did after consultation and due and proper consideration, proceed to formulate a plan of, and take preliminary steps for, the institution and organization of a society composed of descendants of soldiers, sailors and patriots of the Revolutionary War, or more specifically understood and known as the War of 1776, whose deeds of valor in the field and services in the Council

Chamber achieved the independence of the Colonies of the United States of America."

At this provisional meeting, Dr. P. W. Randle was elected President. Dr. Randle was born at Sparta, Georgia, November 9th, 1806. His sire was Captain Josias Randle of the Virginia Line, who, for a time, served as Aid-de-camp to General Washington. With his father he removed to Illinois in 1810, and later received his education at Transylvania College, Kentucky. He served with Abraham Lincoln in the Black Hawk War and was a Surgeon in the Mexican War and during the War of the Rebellion. On December 19th, 1849, he arrived at San Francisco in the ship *Arkansas*, and in the latter years of his life was connected with the U. S. Mint at San Francisco, where he died, January 13th, 1884. His remains were committed to mother earth by George H. Thomas Post, No. 2, G. A. R., of which he was a member, in accordance with the ceremonies of the Grand Army of the Republic.

The provisional organization thus initiated, known as the Society of Sons of Revolutionary Sires, was held well in hand, when, on the 26th day of June, 1876, Centennial Year, the following card from a lady whose name is unknown appeared in the *Daily Alta California:*

Editor Alta:

Wouldn't it be a most novel but strikingly interesting idea in the programme of the procession for our City Centennial Celebration, to have represented our grandparents of the Revolution by the grandchildren now living, residents of this city? There might not be a single living son or daughter, but no doubt there might be a score or more of real grandchildren.

Wouldn't it be splendid if enough could be found to represent every State in the Union, to ride in a car sufficiently large to carry them all, each one carrying a small flag with the name of the State they represent, and the car designated "The Revolutionary Grandchildren?"

The writer of this is such an one, an elderly lady 55 years of age. I am the granddaughter and the step-granddaughter of six who passed through that bloody struggle inaugurated by the Declaration, the anniversary of the signing of which we have celebrated for 99 years, and now are about to give unusual eclat to the Centennial Anniversary. Two of those grandparents lived to be 93 and 96 years of age; both received pensions from the U. S. Government; one of them never laid on a bed after that terrible struggle for our liberty, being deprived of that privilege through the asthma contracted from taking colds, sleeping out in snows and rains, suffering and exposure.

If the writer could be transported back to my native home in good old Massachusetts, almost in sight of Plymouth Rock, I could (I think it is so fresh in my memory) put my feet on the very spot where I have stood with one of my grandmothers when she told me there was where my grandfather dropped his plow, rushed into the old farmhouse, shouldered his musket, kissed her and his infant child (which only died two years ago, just 100 years old), mounted his farm nag just unhitched from the plow, and while the terrible sound of the horseman, To Arms! To Arms! was ringing in my grandmother's ears, he was away to Boston as a volunteer. All honor to our glorious, noble grandparents to-day. I could tell many, many incidents that they all have related to me, so green and fresh and heart-stirring to-day to me as when a child I heard them from their own lips, which I have told myself to many a dear little child in this city to try to explain what the 4th of July or Independence means. These things must be kept before the minds of our young and rising generation, for from some of them, at least, must come the future support of the whole fabric so dearly won by those martyred heroes, whose cry—Liberty or Death—went up to the ears of a willing Merciful Father to relieve us from tyranny and oppression, making a home for all to worship as they choose, and to buy, sell and get gain, and send it where they list.

If the General of the day thinks anything of this—for I know you will let him see it—tell him I want to go and carry the old Bay State Flag, my dear native home, which I have not seen for fourteen years. I am the poor widow of one of the victims of the privateers of our last war, living in obscurity.

Yours, etc.,

———————————.

To the unknown correspondent of the *Alta* Dr. Cogswell replied in the following communication:

REVOLUTIONARY DESCENDANTS.

Editor Alta:

The idea suggested by the granddaughter of one of our Revolutionary Sires seems a capital one; and as I belong in the same category with your correspondent, being the grandson of one of the Revolutionary heroes, I shall be happy to have all who belong to this class call at my office, No. 230 Kearny street, and organize for the occasion.

Signed,

J. L. COGSWELL.

San Francisco, June 26th, 1876.

The issue of the *Alta* of June 28th contained the following local item (written by Geo. B. Mackrett, Journalist):

"The grandchildren of Revolutionary Heroes have been invited to meet at the office of Dr. Cogswell, 230 Kearny street, and organize for the proper celebration of the day which their grandfathers fought to make the Republic's great national holiday; and it is not likely that any will be lax in the display of their patriotism through any proper channel that may be open to them. This is the time to arouse the enthusiasm and fire the patriotism of every son of freedom."

Pursuant to the call, a number of descendants of Revolutionary soldiers and sailors convened at the office of Dr. Cogswell, and agreed to connect themselves with the Society "planned and formulated" on the previous 22nd day of October, 1875, and to participate in the Centennial Anniversary of American Independence, the celebration of the day having been entrusted to a General Committee of leading citizens of San Francisco. At the request of the assembled Revolutionary descendants the Grand Marshal issued the following invitation:

1776.   1876.
ATTENTION DESCENDANTS OF REVOLUTIONARY PATRIOTS!
Headquarters Centennial Committee, 212 Kearny Street.

SAN FRANCISCO, June 28th, 1876.
You are hereby requested to meet at the Headquarters of the Grand Marshal, No. 212 Kearny Street, at 8 o'clock P. M., on Thursday, June 29th, for the purpose of making arrangements to participate in the celebration of the One Hundredth Anniversary of the Nation's Independence.   CHARLES L. WIGGIN,
Chief of Staff to the Grand Marshal.

On the same date of the issuance of the above invitation, the *Alta*, through its local column, called attention of descendants of Revolutionary Sires to the approaching celebration in these words:

"The descendants of the Revolutionary patriots in this city are requested to meet at Headquarters of the Grand Marshal, No. 212 Kearny street, at eight o'clock this evening, for the purpose of making arrangements to participate in the Centennial Celebration."

The foregoing request met with a hearty response, there being present about twenty-five persons claiming the distinction and honor of being enrolled as descendants of Revolutionary Sires, and arrangements were perfected for having a parade on Independence Day following. An adjournment to meet at the Palace Hotel Saturday evening, July 1st, was then taken.

At the adjourned meeting the action to have a parade on July 4th was concurred in by almost thirty additional eligibles for membership who were present, the whole forming a nucleus for a promising parade on Independence Day. When the glorious day arrived, there were no less than eighty-eight names enrolled, eight of whom were actual Sons of Revolutionary Soldiers; but at the present writing only one of these—John R. Robinson—is borne on the rolls. Since that date two more have been enrolled, John C. B. Rutherford and Milton Andros.

The parade attracted a great deal of attention, the line of march starting from the Palace Hotel at 9:30 A. M. and passing through the principal streets, everywhere receiving that homage which would naturally fall to the descendants of those whose services destroyed the yoke of tyranny and made the glorious Stars and Stripes the symbol of a land of freedom in perpetuity. After the parade the little band returned to the Palace Hotel and there joined in, and more fully completed its organization as planned and formulated October 22nd, 1875.

Now a word as to the objects of this society. From its very inspiration the promoters of the California Society planned that the organization should be made *National* in its attributes, and among other objects its first constitution provided for the organization of " auxiliaries, co-equal branches and representative bodies." The California organization was perfected July 4, 1876, or seven years prior to the formation of any similar organization in any State in the Union.

This plain statement of existing facts should forever set at rest its claim for dominance in point of life, and as all permanent bodies must possess parentage, so did the California organization become the sire of all assimilated branches and will forever remain as such—despite all quibbling to the contrary.

The National Society early recognized the services of the California Society, by the adoption of, at the first National Congress, at Louisville, Ky., April 30, 1890, the following resolution:

" *Whereas*, The Society of the Sons of the American Revolution was first organized in the State of California on the Fourth of July, 1876 ; and

Whereas, To Colonel A. S. Hubbard, of the California Society, is due, in a large degree, the credit of organizing that Society, and, in a still greater degree, the credit of maintaining that Society through trials which would have discouraged a less patriotic man ; now, therefore,

Resolved, That in the publication of the names of the Presidents-General of the National Society of the Sons of the American Revolution, the name of Colonel A. S. Hubbard be hereafter included.

Resolved, That the Secretary General be, and is hereby, instructed to inform Colonel A. S. Hubbard of the honor which this Congress has conferred upon him.

At the third National Congress, at New York City, April 30, 1892, on motion of Mr. Henry Hall, Historian General, it placed on record the following tribute to the memory of the late General Albert M. Winn:

Resolved, That the name of A. M. Winn, first President of the California Society, shall hereafter appear in the roll of Past Presidents-General of this Society.

CONSTITUTION AND BY-LAWS

California Society of the

Sons of the American Revolution.

PREAMBLE.

CALIFORNIA SOCIETY OF THE SONS OF THE AMERICAN REVOLUTION. Instituted October 22nd, 1875. The first body in inception, institution and organization, to unite the descendants of Revolutionary patriots and perpetuate the memory of *all* those who took part in the American Revolution and maintained the Independence of the United States of America. It was fully and completely organized on the 4th of July, 1876, under the name of "SONS OF REVOLUTIONARY SIRES." On the 30th of April, 1889, a number of similar co-equal Societies of different States formed a general Society under the name of "THE NATIONAL SOCIETY OF THE SONS OF THE AMERICAN REVOLUTION," in which movement this Society heartily co-operated and changed its name to the California Society of the Sons of the American Revolution, under which latter name it has been since known.

Constitution.

ARTICLE I.
NAME.

SECTION 1. The name of this Society is "THE CALIFORNIA SOCIETY OF THE SONS OF THE AMERICAN REVOLUTION."

ARTICLE II.
OBJECTS.

SECTION 1. The objects of this Society shall be to unite and promote fellowship among the descendants, and perpetuate the memory of the men who, by their services or sacrifices during the War of the American Revolution, achieved the independence of the American people; to inspire among the members of the Society and the community at large a more profound reverence for the principles of the Government founded by our forefathers; to encourage historical research in relation to the American Revolution; to acquire and preserve the records of the individual services of Revolutionary patriots, and documents, relics and landmarks connected with the War; to mark the scenes of the Revolution by appropriate memorials; to celebrate the anniversaries of the prominent events of the War; to maintain and extend the institutions of American freedom; and to carry out the injunctions of Washington in his farewell address to the American people.

ARTICLE III.
MEMBERSHIP.

SECTION 1. Any man shall be eligible to membership in this Society, who, being of the age of 21 years or over, and a citizen of good repute in the community, is the lineal descendant of an ancestor, who, while at all times unfailing in his loyalty, rendered actual service in the cause of American Independence, either as an officer, soldier, seaman, marine, militiaman or minute man, in the armed forces of the Continental Congress or of any one of the several Colonies or States; or as a Signer of the Declaration of Independence; or as a member of a Committee of Safety or Correspondence; or as a member of any Continental, Provincial or Colonial Congress or Legislature; or as a civil officer, either of one of the Colonies or States or of the National Government; or as a recognized patriot, who performed actual service by overt acts of rebellion against the authority of Great Britain.

ARTICLE IV.
OFFICERS.

SECTION 1. The officers of the Society shall be a President, a Senior Vice-President, a Junior Vice-President, a Secretary, a Treasurer, a Registrar, a Marshal and a Board of Managers consisting of the above mentioned and six other members, who shall be elected by a vote of the majority of the members present at the annual meeting of the Society, and who shall hold office for one year or until their successors shall be elected.

SEC. 2. Delegates and alternates to the Congress of the National Society shall be elected at the same meeting.

ARTICLE V.
MEETINGS.

SECTION 1. The regular meetings of the Society shall be on the second Tuesday in January; on the nineteenth of April, "Lexington Day;" on the seventeenth of June, "Bunker Hill Day;" on the third of September, the anniversary of the Treaty of Paris, whereby King George III acknowledged the United States of America to be free, sovereign and independent States; on the 19th of October, the anniversary of the surrender of the British Army to the allied armies at Yorktown, except when either of these dates shall fall on Sunday, in which case the meeting shall be held on the day preceding.

SEC. 2. The meeting of the second Tuesday in January shall be the annual meeting, at which, in addition to the transaction of general business, the election of officers for the ensuing year shall take place, who shall hold office for one year or until their successors shall be elected, and shall enter upon their official duty immediately.

SEC. 3. Special meetings may be called by the President or Board of Managers at any time.

SEC. 4. The President shall call a special meeting whenever requested in writing so to do by five or more members.

SEC. 5. No business shall be transacted at any special meeting excepting that for which the meeting was called, unless by a two-thirds vote of the members present.

ARTICLE VI.
AMENDMENTS.

SECTION 1. Amendments to this Constitution must be submitted in writing at a regular meeting of the Society, but shall not be acted on until the next or a subsequent meeting.

SEC. 2. A copy of every proposed amendment shall be sent to each member, with a notice of the meeting at which the same is to be acted on, at least one week prior to said meeting.

SEC. 3. A vote of two-thirds of those present shall be necessary to the adoption of any amendment.

By=Laws.

Section 1. All applications for membership in this Society shall be made in duplicate upon blanks prescribed by the National Society, to which the applicant shall have made oath that the statements of his application are true to the best of his knowledge and belief, and shall be accompanied by the membership fee for the current year within which the application is presented, which shall be returned if the applicant is not accepted.

Sec. 2. No application for membership shall be received wherein the applicant does not clearly establish direct lineal descent from an ancestor who participated in establishing American Independence, as required by Article III of the Constitution.

Sec. 3. Applications for membership shall be received by the Secretary, submitted to the Registrar for examination, and shall be reported by the latter to the Board of Managers for action. When approved and elected by said Board, the applicant shall become a member of the Society. One copy of each application shall be retained by the Registrar for preservation, and the duplicate forwarded to the Registrar-General of the National Society.

Sec. 4. 1. The membership fee shall be ten (10) dollars, and the yearly dues shall be at the rate of twenty-five (25) cents per month. The payment of fifty dollars by a member at any one time, or the payment of annual dues for thirty consecutive years, shall constitute the person paying such sum a life member, and he shall thereafter be exempt from the payment of annual dues.

2. Annual dues shall be paid in advance to the Secretary on or before the day of the annual election. Any member in arrears for dues for two years shall be liable to suspension

and may be dropped by the Board of Managers, but may be re-instated on payment of all arrearages and one (1) year's additional dues, provided he has been suspended for twelve months or more, and provided there are no charges unbecoming a gentleman recorded against him remaining undetermined, or determined finally against him.

3. In extreme cases the Board of Managers may by vote remit the unpaid annual dues of a delinquent member.

SEC. 5. Sons of those who actually participated in the War of the Revolution, and thereby assisted in establishing American Independence, as referred to in Article III of the Constitution, may be admitted to full membership in this Society without payment of membership fee or yearly dues, they having complied with all the other requirements of those belonging to a later generation.

SEC. 6. Honorary membership may be conferred upon the Governor and ex-Governors of the State of California and upon distinguished individuals for services rendered in the Army or Navy of the United States, or for contributions to the Society, who shall not be subject to dues or entitled to vote or hold office, but may take part in debate and be entitled to the honors of re-unions and celebrations, provided they are eligible to membership in the Society.

SEC. 7. The President, or in his absence the Senior Vice-President, or in his absence the Junior Vice-President, or in his absence a Chairman pro tempore, shall preside at all meetings of the Society and of the Board of Managers. He shall enforce a strict observance of the Constitution and By-Laws, and perform such other duties as custom and parliamentary usage may require.

SEC. 8. 1. The Secretary shall receive all moneys from the members and pay them over to the Treasurer, taking his receipt for the same. He shall conduct the general correspondence of the Society, shall have charge of the seal, certificate of incorporation, by-laws and records, and, together with the presiding officer, shall certify all acts of the Society.

2. He shall keep fair and accurate records of all proceedings and orders of the Society, and shall give notice to the several officers of all votes, orders, resolves or proceedings affecting them or appertaining to their respective duties.

3. He shall notify all members of their election, and shall, under the direction of the President, give due notice of the time and place of all meetings of the Society and attend the same.

4. He shall keep a true account of his receipts and payments, and of the accounts of the members with the Society, and at each annual meeting shall report the same, at which time a committee shall be appointed to audit his accounts.

Sec. 9. The Treasurer shall receive from the Secretary all moneys belonging to the Society, giving his receipt for the same; these funds shall be deposited in a reliable bank or savings institution in the city of San Francisco, to be designated by the Board of Managers, to the credit of "The California Society of the Sons of the American Revolution," and shall be drawn thence on the check of the Treasurer for the use of the Society only, as directed by vote of the Society or by the Board of Managers, upon the order of the Secretary and the certificate of the President. He shall keep a true account of his receipts and payments and at each annual meeting shall report the same, at which time a committee shall be appointed to audit his accounts.

Sec. 10. 1. The Registrar shall keep a roll of members, and in his hands shall be lodged all proofs of membership-qualification, and the historical and genealogical papers—manuscript or otherwise—of which the Society may become possessed; and under the direction of the Board of Managers shall keep copies of such similar documents as the owners thereof may not be willing to leave permanently in the keeping of the Society. He shall receive all applications for membership and proofs of membership-qualifications from the Secretary, shall carefully scrutinize and verify all statements of the Revolutionary services of ancestors that may be made in the applications, and shall report his findings in each case to the Board of Managers.

Sec. 11. 1. The Board of Managers shall consist of thirteen members, viz: the President, Senior and Junior Vice-Presidents, Secretary, Treasurer, Registrar, Marshal ex-officio, and six others, elected as provided by the Constitution.

2. They shall judge of the qualifications of the candidates for admission to the Society and elect the same, two negative votes rejecting the applicant.

3. They shall recommend plans for promoting the objects of the Society, shall digest and prepare business, and shall authorize the disbursement and expenditure of unappropriated money in the treasury for the payment of current expenses of the Society. They shall generally superintend the interests of the Society, and perform all such duties as may be committed to them by the Society.

4. They shall have power to fill any vacancy occurring or existing in the Society, and an officer so appointed shall act until the following annual election or until his successor shall be chosen.

5. At each annual meeting of the Society the Board shall make a general report.

6. At all meetings of the Board of Managers five or more shall be sufficient for the transaction of business.

Sec. 12. The seal of this Society shall be the same as that of the "National Society of the Sons of the American Revolution, organized April 30th, 1889," with the addition of an inner circle, three-sixteenths of an inch wide, bearing the following legend: "California Society, S. A. R.; organized July 4th, 1876."

Sec. 13. No alteration or amendment of the By-Laws of this Society shall be made unless openly proposed at a previous meeting and entered in the minutes with the name of the member proposing the same, and shall be adopted by a majority of the members present at a meeting of the Society.

In Memoriam

Rev. Chas. Morris Blake, U. S. A.

Rev. Benj. F. Crary, D. D.

Genl. Wm. H. Dimond.

Hon. Chas. Fernald.

Arthur Malise Heanan.

James L. Halsted, Sr.

Charles B. Kimball.

Henry McLean Martin.

David Meeker, Sr.

N. Valentine Paddock.

James McM. Shafter.

Capt. A. C. Taylor.

William Winter.

Col. David Wilder.

Col. Uriah Wallace.

Capt. S. G. Whipple, U. S. A.

Benjamin F. Williams.

Roll of Membership.

ABBOTT, CARL HEWES. Oakland.
> Great-great-grandson of Walter Fanning, Private Connecticut Militia.

ABBOTT, GEORGE EDWARDS, M. D. San Diego.
> Great-grandson of Joshua Abbott, Captain Continental Army, New Hampshire Line.

ABBOTT, GRANVILLE DAVIS. Oakland.
> Great-great-grandson of Walter Fanning, Private Connecticut Militia.

ALLEN, CHARLES R. Oakland.
> Great-grandson of John Wilbur, Private Rhode Island Troops.

ALLEN, EDGAR L. San Francisco.
> Great-grandson of John Wilbur, Private Rhode Island Troops.

ANDERSON, CHARLES, M. D. Santa Barbara.
> Grandson of Richard Clough Anderson, Lieutenant-Colonel Continental Army, Virginia Line.

ANDREWS, REV. J. B. San Jose.
> Grandson of Conrad Rummey, Private Pennsylvania Troops.

ANDROS, MILTON. San Francisco.
> Son of Rev. Thomas Andros, Private Continental Army.

AUSTIN, CHARLES GOODRIDGE. San Francisco.
> Great-grandson of Levi Austin;
> *Also*, Great-grandson of Daniel Goodridge, Privates Massachusetts Militia.

AYER, LEONARD BARNARD. Central House.

Great-grandson of William Ayer, Private Massachusetts Militia.

BABCOCK, GEORGE REED. Oakland.

Great-great-great-grandson of Benjamin Franklin, Signer of the Declaration of Independence. Member Continental Congress. Minister to France.

BACKUS, GENERAL SAMUEL WOOLSEY. San Francisco.

Great-grandson of Moses Nichols, Colonel New Hampshire Troops.

BAILEY, JAMES DYAS. San Francisco.

Great-grandson of Paul Bailey, Captain of Coast Guards, Massachusetts Militia.

BAKER, FREDERICK, M. D. San Diego.

Great-grandson of John Raymond, Lieutenant Connecticut Troops.

BALDWIN, FREDERICK ALBERT. San Francisco.

Great-great-grandson of Moses Hall, Sergeant Massachusetts Militia.

BARKER, TIMOTHY LEONARD. Oakland.

Grandson of Timothy Barker;
Also, Grandson of Justin Leonard, Privates Massachusetts Troops.

BARTLETT, COLUMBUS. Alameda.

Great-grandson of Stephen Bartlett, Lieutenant New Hampshire Militia;
Also, Great-great-grandson of Asa Bailey, Major New Hampshire Troops.

BARTLETT, LOUIS DE FONTENAY. Alameda.

Great-great-grandson of Stephen Bartlett, Lieutenant New Hampshire Militia;
Also, Great-great-great-grandson of Asa Bailey, Major New Hampshire Troops.

BELLOWS, EDWARD, U. S. N. Walpole, N. H.

Great-grandson of Joseph Bellows, Lieutenant-Colonel Massachusetts Militia.

BERRY, COLONEL JOHN RIDDELL. Los Angeles.
> Great-grandson of John Berry, Private Pennsylvania Troops.

BIGELOW, CHARLES E. Santa Barbara.
> Great-grandson of John Richardson, Member of the General Court (Massachusetts). Captain Massachusetts Militia.

BLACKWOOD, NORMAN JEROME, M. D., U. S. N.
> Great - great - grandson of Ephraim Kirby, Ensign Rhode Island Troops.

*BLAKE, REV. CHARLES MORRIS.
> Grandson of John Blake, Lieutenant Massachusetts Troops.

BOARDMAN, GEORGE CHAUNCEY. San Francisco.
> Grandson of Oliver Boardman;
> *Also*, Grandson of Abel Lewis, Privates Connecticut Militia.

BOARDMAN, SAMUEL HORT. San Francisco.
> Great-grandson of Oliver Boardman;
> *Also*, Great-grandson of Abel Lewis, Privates Connecticut Militia.

BOARDMAN, THOMAS DANFORTH. San Francisco.
> Great-grandson of Oliver Boardman;
> *Also*, Great-grandson of Abel Lewis, Privates Connecticut Militia.

BONNELL, EDWIN. Berkeley.
> Grandson of Aaron Bonnell;
> *Also*, Great-grandson of Othneil Looker, Privates New Jersey Militia.

BOOTH, LUCIUS A. Piedmont.
> Grandson of Walter Booth, Sergeant Connecticut Militia.

BRANDEGEE, TOWNSHEND STICH. San Diego.
> Great-grandson of Elisharan Brandegee, Private Connecticut Troops.

BROMLEY, JOHN LEWIS. Oakland.
> Great-grandson of William Bromley, Member of the Committee of Safety, Danbury, Vt.

BROMLEY, ROBERT INNIS, M. D Sonora.

> Great-great-grandson of William Bromley, Member of the
> Committee of Safety, Danbury, Vt.

BROWN, PHILIP KING, M. D. San Francisco.

> Great-great-grandson of John Blake, Lieutenant Massa-
> chusetts Troops.

BROWN, ROBERT TURNBULL. San Francisco.

> Great-grandson of Seth Hooker, Private Massachusetts
> Militia.

BUNKER, WILLIAM MITCHELL. San Francisco.

> Great-grandson of John Morris, Seaman Brigantine *Lucy*,
> U. S. N.

BURBECK, EDWARD MITCHELL. San Diego.

> Great-great-grandson of William Burbeck, Colonel Conti-
> nental Army;
> *Also*, Great-grandson of Edward Burbeck, Captain Continental
> Army, Massachusetts Line.

BURBECK, LUCIUS DOOLITTLE. San Diego.

> Great-great-grandson of William Burbeck, Colonel Conti-
> nental Army;
> *Also*, Great-grandson of Edward Burbeck, Captain Continental
> Army, Massachusetts Line.

BURNETT, LESTER GRANT. San Francisco.

> Great-grandson of Solomon Cleveland, Private Connecticut
> Militia;
> *Also*, Great-grandson of James Burnett, Sergeant Connecticut
> Militia.

BURNETT, CAPT. WELLINGTON CLEVELAND. San Francisco.

> Grandson of James Burnett, Private Connecticut Militia.

BURNHAM, CLARK JAMES, M. D. San Francisco.

> Great-grandson of James Burnham, Captain Massachusetts
> Troops;
> *Also*, Great-great-grandson of Seth Burnham, Private Massa-
> chusetts Troops.

BURT, JOHN PEEK. San Diego.

> Grandson of David Burt, Lieutenant Massachusetts Militia.

BURTON, HENRY G., M. D. San Diego.

> Great-grandson of Elijah Burton, Private Vermont Militia;
> *Also*, Great-grandson of Josiah Graves, Private New York Militia.

CARNES, WALTER. San Diego.

> Great-great-grandson of John Frost, Brigadier-General Massachusetts Troops.

CATLIN, ALEXANDER DONALDSON. Sacramento.

> Great-grandson of David Catlin, Lieutenant Connecticut Militia;
> *Also*, Great-grandson of Zebulon Butler, Colonel Continental Army, Connecticut Line.

CATLIN, HON. AMOS PARMALEE. Sacramento

> Grandson of David Catlin, Lieutenant Connecticut Militia.

CHANNING, GIOVANNI EUGENE. San Francisco.

> Great-great-grandson of William Ellery, Signer Declaration of Independence. Member of Continental Congress.

CLARK, EDWARD STEPHENS, M. D. San Francisco.

> Great-great-grandson of Stephen Clark, Captain New Hampshire Militia.

CLARK, LEONARD STOCKWELL. San Francisco.

> Great-grandson of John Stockwell, Private Massachusetts Militia.

CLEVELAND, HON. DANIEL. San Diego.

> Grandson of Stephen Cleveland;
> *Also*, Great-grandson of James Huntington, Sergeants Connecticut Troops.

COGSWELL, THOMAS. San Diego.

> Grandson of William Cogswell, Surgeon's Mate Connecticut Line, Continental Army.

COLLIER, ROBERT O. San Francisco.

> Great-great-great-grandson of Israel Putnam, Major-General Continental Army.

CORLISS, CAPTAIN AUGUSTUS W., U. S. A. Fort Logan, Colo.
Great-grandson of Joshua Corliss, Private Massachusetts
Troops.

CRANE, ALPHONSE. Santa Barbara.
Great-grandson of Simeon Stedman, Private Massachusetts
Militia.

*CRARY, REV. BENJAMIN FRANKLIN, D. D.
Grandson of John Crary, Private New York Troops.

CROCKER, COLONEL CHARLES FREDERICK. San Francisco.
Great-great-grandson of Seth Read, Lieutenant-Colonel
Continental Army, Massachusetts Line.

CROCKER, HENRY GRAHAM. Coronado.
Great-great-great-grandson of Isaac Cook, Jr., Lieutenant-
Colonel Continental Army.

CROCKER, WILLIAM HENRY. San Francisco.
Great-great-grandson of Seth Read, Lieutenant-Colonel
Continental Army, Massachusetts Line.

CURRIER, COLONEL JOHN CHARLES. San Francisco.
Grandson of David Currier, Sergeant New Hampshire
Militia.

CUTLER, COLONEL ALFRED DENNIS. San Francisco.
Great-grandson of Ammi Cutler, Private Massachusetts
Militia;
Also, Grandson of Thomas Cutler, Private Massachusetts Militia.

CUTTER, EDWARD B. San Francisco.
Great-great-grandson of Samuel Cutter, Lieutenant Conti-
nental Army, Massachusetts Line;
Also, Great-great-great-grandson of Samuel Whittemore, Captain
Massachusetts Militia.

CUTTING, GENERAL JOHN TYLER. New York City.
Great-grandson of Jonas Cutting, Sergeant New Hampshire
Militia.

DAGGETT, HENRY. San Diego.

>Great-grandson of Rev. Naphthali Daggett, President Yale College. Died of wounds received in Volunteer Service.

DANFORTH, EDWIN. San Francisco.

>Grandson of William Danforth, Drummer and Corporal Massachusetts Militia.

DAVIS, HON. HORACE. San Francisco.

>Grandson of Isaac Davis, Lieutenant Massachusetts Line;
>*Also,* Grandson of Aaron Bancroft, Private Massachusetts Militia.

DAY, FRANKLIN HENRY. San Francisco.

>Great-grandson of Eli Root, Captain Massachusetts Militia.

DAYTON, LIEUTENANT JOHN HAVENS. U. S. N.

>Great-great-grandson of John Dayton, Captain New York Militia.

DIMOND, EDWIN RODOLPH. San Francisco.

>Great-great-grandson of Daniel Dimon, Ensign Connecticut Militia.

* DIMOND, MAJOR-GENERAL WILLIAM HENRY.

>Great - grandson of Daniel Dimon, Ensign Connecticut Militia.

DINSMORE, REV. JOHN WALKER, D. D. San Jose.

>Grandson of James Anderson, Captain Pennsylvania Troops.

DODGE, ZENAS UPHAM. San Francisco.

>Great-grandson of Samuel Upham, Private Massachusetts Militia.

DONOHOE, JR., DENIS. San Rafael.

>Great-great-grandson of William Barton, Colonel Continental Army, Rhode Island Line.

DORR, LEVI LEWIS, M. D. San Francisco.

>Great - grandson of Luke Perkins, Private Massachusetts Militia.

LIEUT. ISAAC DAVIS
6TH MASS. REGIMENT

FEBRUARY 27TH, 1749   APRIL 27TH, 1826

DU BOIS, PIERRE CHEASMAN. San Francisco.

Great-grandson of Peter Du Bois, Private New York Levies;

Also, Great-grandson of Enoch Smith, Private Connecticut Militia;

Also, Great - grandson of Ralph Schenck, Private New York Levies.

DUNBAR, REV. GEORGE WARD, U. S. A. Janesville, Wis.

Great-grandson of Josiah Jewett, Captain Connecticut Militia.

DUTTON, SAMUEL EDWARDS. San Francisco.

Great-grandson of Samuel Dutton, Private Massachusetts Militia.

EASTIN, WILLIAM BOARDMAN. San Francisco.

Grandson of William Eastin, Sergeant Virginia Militia.

EVERTS, EDWARD, M. D., U. S. A. Whipple Barracks, Ariz.

Grandson of Ambrose Everts, Private Connecticut Militia.

FARRINGTON, J. W. Alameda.

Great-grandson of Josiah Farrington, Private Massachusetts Militia.

*FERNALD, HON. CHARLES.

Grandson of Hercules Archelaus Fernald, Private Massachusetts Militia.

FINCH, WILLIAM HENEAGE. San Francisco.

Great-grandson of John Finch, Lieutenant New York Militia.

FLINT, HON. THOMAS, JR. North San Juan.

Great-grandson of Thomas Flint, Surgeon U. S. N.;

Also, Daniel Wilkins, Captain Continental Army, New Hampshire Line.

FOLSOM, GEORGE THORNDIKE. San Francisco.

Great-great-grandson of Jonathan Folsom, Lieutenant New Hampshire Militia;

Also, Great-grandson of Benjamin Folsom, Private New Hampshire Militia.

FRANKLIN, WILLIAM SEWARD. San Francisco.
>Great-grandson of Peleg Slade, Lieutenant-Colonel Massa-
chusetts Militia.

GEORGE, WILLIAM H., M. D. Bishop, Cal.
>Grandson of Jesse George, Private Virginia Militia.

GOSS, ALFRED FURBUSH. San Francisco.
>Grandson of Josiah Abbott, Lieutenant Continental Army,
Massachusetts Line.

GRAY, ADONIRAM JUDSON. San Diego.
>Great - grandson of Isaiah Gray, Private Massachusetts
Troops.

GRAY, ROSCOE SPAULDING. Oakland.
>Great-grandson of John Gray, Member of the Committee
of Safety, Kings District, N. Y.

GREENAWALT, LORENZO LEONARD. San Diego.
>Great - grandson of Philip Lorenz Greenawalt, Colonel
Pennsylvania Militia.

GREENE, CARLTON WEBSTER. Oakland.
>Great-great-grandson of Thomas Green;
>*Also,* Great-great-grandson of Abiathar Green;
>*Also,* Great-great-grandson of Aaron Childs, Privates Massachu-
setts Militia.

GREENE, CHARLES SAMUEL. Oakland.
>Great-grandson of Christopher Greene, Member of the Com-
mittee of Public Safety. Commander of Kentish Guards;
>*Also,* Great-great-grandson of Governor Samuel Ward of Rhode
Island, Delegate to Continental Congress, 1775;
>*Also,* Great-great-grandson of Nathan Goodale, Major Continental
Army;
>*Also,* Great-grandson of Wanton Casey, Private Kentish Guards.

GREENE, HON. WILLIAM ELLSWORTH. Oakland.
>Great-grandson Thomas Green;
>*Also,* Grandson of Abiathar Green, Privates Massachusetts Mil-
itia.

GRIFFIN, ANDREW G. Alameda.
Great-great-grandson of Robert Hichborn, Lieutenant Massachusetts Militia.

GRIFFIN, CHARLES W. Alameda.
Great-great-grandson of Robert Hichborn, Lieutenant Massachusetts Militia.

GUTHRIE, ARTHUR SMITH. Merced.
Great-great-grandson of Andrew Hazlet, Private Pennsylvania Militia.

HALE, WILLIAM ELMER. San Quentin.
Grandson Dr. William Hale, Surgeon New Hampshire Militia.

HALL, CHARLES LANDER. San Francisco.
Great-grandson of Timothy Hall, Private Connecticut Militia.

HALL, GEORGE ELI. San Francisco.
Great-grandson of Timothy Hall, Private Connecticut Militia.

HALSTEAD, EMINEL POTTER, D. D. S. San Francisco.
Great-grandson of Joseph Halsted, Private Connecticut Militia.

*HALSTED, JAMES LAFAYETTE, SR.
Grandson of Joseph Halsted, Private Connecticut Militia.

HALSTED, JAMES LAFAYETTE, JR. San Francisco.
Great-grandson of Joseph Halsted, Private Connecticut Militia.

HALSTED, JOHN BERNARD. San Francisco.
Great-grandson of Joseph Halsted, Private Connecticut Militia.

HALSTED, WILLIAM AUGUSTUS. San Francisco.
Great-grandson of Joseph Halsted, Private Connecticut Militia.

HARDY, EUGENE ATWOOD. Ætna Mine.

Great-grandson of John Harkness, Lieutenant Continental Army, New Hampshire Line.

HASELTINE, CHARLES EBENEZER. San Francisco.

Grandson of Ebenezer Byram, Private Massachusetts Militia.

HATCH, AUGUSTUS TIMOTHY. San Francisco.

Great - grandson of Moses Porter, Captain Connecticut Militia.

HAVEN, CHARLES DWIGHT. Oakland.

Grandson of Jeremiah Baker, Private Massachusetts Militia; *Also*, Great-grandson of Daniel Whiting, Lieutenant-Colonel Continental Army, Massachusetts Line.

HAWLEY, WALTER AUGUSTUS. Santa Barbara.

Great-great-grandson of Thomas Hawley, Sergeant Connecticut Militia.

HAWXHURST, ROBERT. Alameda.

Great-grandson of Isaac Livingston, Connecticut Militia.

HEAD, ERNEST KNOX. San Francisco.

Great-grandson of General Henry Knox, General Continental Army;
Also, Great-grandson of Nathaniel Head, Captain New Hampshire Militia.

* **HEANAN, ARTHUR MALISE.**

Great-great-great-grandson William Faulkner, Private Pennsylvania Militia.

HEWES, DAVID. San Francisco.

Great-grandson of Gilbert Tapley, Lieutenant Massachusetts Militia;
Also, Grandson of Joseph Tapley, Lieutenant Massachusetts Militia.

HEWES, MARLAND SMITH. Oakland.
> Great-grandson of John Huse, Lieutenant Massachusetts Militia.

HOLDEN, PROFESSOR EDWARD SINGLETON. Mt. Hamilton.
> Great-grandson of Samuel Holden, Captain Massachusetts Troops.

HOLLADAY, EDMUND BURKE. San Francisco.
> Great-grandson of Daniel Cresap, Jr., Lieutenant Maryland Rifles.

HOLLADAY, SAMUEL W. San Francisco.
> Grandson of Samuel Holladay, Private Massachusetts Troops.

HOOPER, MAJOR WILLIAM BURCHELL. San Francisco.
> Grandson of George Hooper, Drummer Connecticut Militia.

HOUGHTON, HON. JAMES FRANKLIN. San Francisco.
> Grandson Benjamin Houghton, Captain Massachusetts Militia.

HOWE, GEORGE E. San Francisco.
> Grandson of Jeremiah Carleton, Lieutenant New Hampshire Troops.

HOWLAND, JAMES LAURISTON. Pomona.
> Great-great-grandson of Eliphalet Thorp, Captain Massachusetts Militia.

HUBBARD, COLONEL ADOLPHUS SKINNER. San Francisco.
> Great-grandson of Ensign Peter Hubbard, Jr., New Hampshire Militia;
> *Also*, Great-grandson Elijah Ward, Private Massachusetts Line, Continental Army;
> *Also*, Great-grandson Jeremiah Wilson, Private New Hampshire Militia;
> *Also*, Great-grandson of Isaac Clark, Lieutenant New Hampshire Troops.

HUBBARD, THEODORE WORTHINGTON. Chicago, Ill.

> Great-great-grandson of Peter Hubbard, Jr., Ensign New Hampshire Militia;
>
> *Also*, Great-great-grandson of Elijah Ward, Private Continental Army, Massachusetts Line;
>
> *Also*, Great-great-grandson of Jeremiah Wilson, Private New Hampshire Militia;
>
> *Also*, Great-great-grandson of Isaac Clark, Lieutenant New Hampshire Militia;
>
> *Also*, Great-grandson of Valentine Holt, Private New Hampshire Militia.

HUBBELL, CHARLES. San Diego.

> Grandson of Abijah Hubbell, Corporal Connecticut Troops;
>
> *Also*, Great-grandson of Gershom Hubbell, Connecticut Troops.

HUIE, WILLIAM HENRY THOMPSON. San Francisco.

> Great-grandson of Philip Slaughter, Captain Virginia Riflemen.
>
> *Also*, Great-great-grandson of James Slaughter, Member Committee of Safety, Culpeper County, Virginia. Colonel Virginia Militia.

HUNTER, LIEUT.-COL. EDWARD, U. S. A. St. Paul, Minn.

> Great-grandson of James Hunter, Colonel Massachusetts Troops.

HUNTER, HENRY HOFF. St. Paul, Minn.

> Great-great-great-grandson of Kilian Van Rensselaer, Colonel New York Troops.

HUTCHINSON, CHARLES TRIPLER. Alameda.

> Great-great-grandson of Thomas Hunt, Colonel Continental Army, Massachusetts Line.

JACKSON, SEYMOUR HATHAWAY. Oakland.

> Grandson of James Jackson, Lieutenant New York Levies.

JARBOE, PAUL R. San Francisco.

> Great-great-grandson of Malachi Thomas, Sergeant New York Levies;
>
> *Also*, Great-great-great-grandson of David Smith, Lieutenant;
>
> *Also*, Great-great-great-grandson of Eleazar Cady, Private Connecticut Militia.

JONES, HARRISON ALEXANDER. San Francisco.
> Great-great-grandson of Dr. Claiborne Vaughan, Surgeon Continental Army, Virginia Line.

KEELER, BURR BRADLEY. San Francisco.
> Great-grandson of Phillip Burr Bradley, Colonel Connecticut Troops.

KELLOGG, SHELDON INGALLS, JR. Oakland.
> Great-grandson of Phineas Kellogg, Private Connecticut Militia.

*KIMBALL, CHARLES BRADBURY.
> Great-grandson of John Kimball, Private Massachusetts Militia.

KIMBALL, RAY THURSTON. San Francisco.
> Great-grandson of Reuben Kimball, Captain New Hampshire Militia.

KING, CHARLES JAMES. San Francisco.
> Great-grandson of John Libbey, Private New Hampshire Militia;
> *Also*, Great-grandson of John De Mier, Captain New York Levies.

KING, WILLIAM NEIL. San Diego.
> Great-grandson of Rufus King, Major and Aid-de-camp Continental Army.

KNIGHT, ALLEN. San Francisco.
> Great-grandson of Allen Hancock, Corporal Massachusetts Militia.

LADD, FRANK BACON. San Francisco.
> Great-great-grandson of Timothy Dimock, Private Connecticut Militia.

LATHROP, CHARLES GARDNER. San Francisco.
> Grandson of Jedediah Lathrop, Private Connecticut Militia;
> *Also*, Grandson of Daniel Shields, Private New York Levies.

LAUMAN, GEORGE. Spokane, Wash.
>Great-grandson of Christopher Lauman, Lieutenant Pennsylvania Troops.

LEWIS, WILLIAM FRISBIE, M D. Oakland.
>Grandson of William Frisbey, Private New York Militia;
>*Also*, Great-grandson of Thomas Davidson, Member Committee of Safety;
>*Also*, Great-grandson of John Lewis, Private New York Militia;
>*Also*, Great-grandson of John Gunsaul, Private New York Troops.

LOCKWOOD, CAPT. JOHN ALEXANDER, U. S. A. San Francisco.
>Great-great-grandson of George Read, Signer of the Declaration of Independence;
>*Also*, Great-grandson of Allan McLane, Lieutenant Continental Army, Delaware Line.

MANNING, HORATIO SEYMOUR. San Francisco.
>Great-grandson of Nathaniel Manning, Private Connecticut Militia.

*MARTIN, HENRY MAC LEAN.
>Great-great-grandson of Josiah Crosby, Captain New Hampshire Troops.

MASTICK, SEABURY CONE. New York City.
>Great-grandson of Benjamin Mastick, Private Massachusetts Militia.

MATHEWS, HENRY EDWARD. San Francisco.
>Great-grandson of David Hollister, Drummer;
>*Also*, Great-grandson Jason Kellogg, Private Connecticut Militia.

MAUZY, BYRON. San Francisco.
>Great-grandson of William Mauzy, Private Virginia Militia.

McHENRY, JOHN. San Francisco.
>Great-grandson of Jesse McHenry, Private Virginia Militia.

McKEE, JAMES ROBERT. Bardsdale.

Great-grandson of John Mills, Captain Virginia Troops;
Also, Great-grandson of William McClintock, Private Virginia
Militia;
Also, Great-grandson of John McKee, Private South Carolina
Militia.

McKINSTRY, HON. ELISHA WILLIAMS. San Francisco.

Grandson of Charles McKinstry, Lieutenant New York
Levies;
Also, Great-grandson of Gamaliel Whiting, Lieutenant Conti-
nental Army, Massachusetts Line.

McKINSTRY, J. C. San Francisco.

Great-grandson of Charles McKinstry, Lieutenant New York
Levies;
Also, Great-great-grandson of Gamaliel Whiting, Lieutenant Con-
tinental Army, Massachusetts Line;
Also, Great-great-great-grandson of David Milford, Colonel New
York Militia;
Also, Great-great-great-great-grandson of Robert Livingston, a
patriot of New York.

MEAD, WILLIAM H. San Francisco.

Great-grandson of John Paulding, one of the capturers of
Major André.

*MEEKER, DAVID, SR.

Grandson of Obadiah Meeker, Lieutenant New Jersey
Militia.

MOODY, FREDERICK SCHANDER. San Francisco.

Great-great-great-grandson of John DeBow, Captain;
Also, Great-great-great-grandson of Simon Van Ness, Lieutenant
New Jersey Militia.

MOORE, JOHN W., U. S. N. Brooklyn, N. Y.

Great-grandson of Benjamin Mooers, Lieutenant;
Also, Grandson of Pliny Moore, Lieutenant;
Also, Great-great-grandson of Zephaniah Platt, Colonel;
Also, Great-grandson of Nathaniel Platt, Captain New York
Troops.

MORGAN, EDWARD CURRIER. San Diego.

>Great-grandson of Winthrop Sargent, Private Massachusetts Militia.

MOSES, WILLIAM SCHUYLER. San Francisco.

>Grandson of Benjamin Carpenter, New York Militia.

MOULTON, IRVING FARRAR. San Francisco.

>Great-grandson of Brigadier-General Jotham Moulton, York County, Maine, Militia;
>
>*Also*, Great-grandson of Humphrey Farrar, Private Massachusetts Militia;
>
>*Also*, Great-great-grandson of Samuel Farrar, Captain Massachusetts Militia.

MUNGER, LUCIUS AUGUSTUS. Tracy, Cal.

>Great-grandson of James Munger, Captain Connecticut Militia.

NASON, ARTHUR GRAHAM. San Diego.

>Great-grandson of Isaac Gates, Captain Massachusetts Militia.

NASON, MALCOLM CRAIG. San Diego.

>Great-grandson of Isaac Gates, Captain Massachusetts Militia.

NEWCOMB, BETHUEL M. Oat Hill.

>Great-grandson of Nathaniel Shaw, Private Massachusetts Militia.

NORCROSS, DANIEL. San Francisco.

>Grandson of John Norcross, New Jersey Militia.

NORTH, HART HYATT. San Francisco.

>Great-great-grandson of Benjamin North, Lieutenant New York Levies;
>
>*Also*, Great-grandson of Robert North, Sr., Private New York Troops;
>
>*Also*, Great-great-grandson of John Carter, Captain Connecticut Militia;
>
>*Also*, Great-great-great-grandson of Luke Remsen, Private New York Levies;

Also, Great-grandson of Joshua Pine, Commissary Continental Army, New Jersey Line;

Also, Great-great-grandson of Silas Walbridge, Sr., Private Vermont Militia;

Also, Great-great-great-grandson of Rev. Jedediah Dewey, Member Council of Safety, Bennington, Vermont.

NORTON, FRANK BUTLER. San Francisco.
> Great-grandson of Peter Norton, Private Massachusetts Militia.

OLNEY, EDWARD. Oakland.
> Great-great-grandson of Samuel Snow, Captain Rhode Island Militia;
> *Also*, Great-great-grandson of Colonel William Page, Aid-de-camp to General Washington.

ORD, JAMES LYCURGUS, M. D. Monterey.
> Grandson of Daniel Cresap, Jr., Lieutenant Maryland Rifles.

PACK, JOHN W. San Francisco.
> Great-grandson of William Pack, Private New Jersey Troops.

*PADDOCK, N. VALENTINE. San Diego.
> Great-grandson of David Paddock, Private New York Levies.

PAUL, ALMARIN BROOKS, SR. San Francisco.
> Grandson of Almarin Brooks, Sr., Lieutenant New Jersey Troops.

PAYSON, ALBERT HENRY. San Mateo.
> Great-grandson of Ezra Newhall, Lieutenant-Colonel Continental Army, Massachusetts Line.

PELHAM, JAMES EUBANK, M. D. San Francisco.
> Grandson of Charles Pelham, Major Virginia Militia.

PERKINS, HON. GEORGE CLEMENT. Oakland.
> Grandson of William Fairfield, Private Massachusetts Militia.

PERKINS, THOMAS ALLEN. San Francisco.

> Great-grandson of Jacob Allen, Private New Hampshire Troops.

PHELPS, ALANSON HOSMER. San Francisco.

> Great-grandson of Eliphalet Phelps, Private Connecticut Militia.

PHELPS, JR., LIEUT. THOMAS STOWELL, U. S. N. Mare Island.

> Great-great-grandson of Thomas Nixon, Colonel Continental Army, Massachusetts Line.

PHELPS, WILLIAM SIDNEY. San Francisco.

> Great-grandson of Eliphalet Phelps, Private Connecticut Militia.

PLIMPTON, FREDERIC SANFORD. San Diego.

> Grandson of Elijah Plimpton, Private;
> *Also,* Grandson of Josiah Pratt, Captain Massachusetts Troops.

PLUM, JR., CHARLES MORTIMER. San Francisco.

> Great-grandson of John Plum, Private New York Levies.

POLHEMUS, EDWARD. San Francisco.

> Great-grandson of John Polhemus, Major Continental Army, New Jersey Line.

POSEY, DR. ADDISON C. San Francisco.

> Great-grandson of Thomas Posey, General Continental Army.

PUTMAN, DeWITT C. Santa Monica.

> Great-grandson of Jacob Putman, Jr., Private New York Militia.

PRESSOR, GEORGE R. San Francisco.

> Great-grandson of William Winchester, Lieutenant Continental Army, Massachusetts Line.

RAND, HALL BURGIN. Oakland.

> Grandson of William Rand, Private New Hampshire Militia.

THE UNITED STATES OF AMERICA

IN CONGRESS ASSEMBLED

Greeting.

We, reposing especial trust and confidence in your Patriotism, valour, conduct and fidelity, DO by these presents constitute and appoint you _____ _____ _____ _____ _____ in the army of the United States to take rank as _____ from _____ _____ _____

You are therefore carefully and diligently to discharge the duty of _____ by doing and performing all manner of things thereunto belonging. And we do strictly charge and require all officers and soldiers under your command, to be obedient to your orders as _____ And you are to observe and follow such orders and directions from time to time as you shall receive from this or a future Congress of the United States, or a Committee of Congress for that purpose appointed, or Commander in chief for the time being of the armies of the United States, or any other your superior Officers, according to the rules and discipline of war, in pursuance of the trust reposed in you. This Commission to continue in force until revoked by this or a future Congress, the Committee of Congress before mentioned, or a Committee of the States.

Witness His Excellency _____ _____ President of the Congress of the United States of America, at _____ the _____ day of _____ _____ present, in the year of our _____ and in the _____ Year of our Independence.

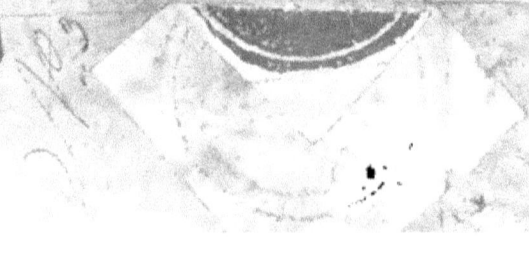

RANDOLPH, REV. THOMAS LYMAN. Alameda.
> Great-grandson of Benjamin Harrison, Signer of the Declaration of Independence and Member of Congress;
> *Also*, Grandson of Daniel Lyman, Colonel Continental Army.

REDINGTON, ALFRED POETT. Santa Barbara.
> Great-grandson of Asa Redington, Corporal New Hampshire Militia.

REED, GEORGE WHITNEY. San Francisco.
> Great-great-grandson of James Reed, Brigadier-General Continental Army.

REED, CAPTAIN WILLIAM I., U. S. A. San Francisco.
> Great-grandson of Jacob Read, Corporal Massachusetts Militia.

REQUA, ISAAC LAWRENCE. San Francisco.
> Great-grandson of Glode Requa, Captain New York Militia.

REQUA, JAMES EDGAR. Sonora.
> Grandson of Abraham Requa;
> *Also*, Great-grandson of Daniel Requa, Private New York Levies.

REQUA, MARK LAWRENCE. San Francisco.
> Great-great-grandson of Glode Requa, Captain New York Militia.

ROBINSON, JOHN ROGERS. San Francisco.
> Son of Noah Robinson, Captain New Hampshire Troops.

ROYCE, CHARLES O. Chico.
> Great-grandson of Jonas Rice, Lieutenant Vermont Troops.

RUTHERFORD, JOHN CHARLES B. Oakland.
> Son of John Rutherford, Private Massachusetts Militia.

SAWYER, CAPTAIN JAMES ESTCOURT, U. S. A. Buffalo, N. Y.
> Great-grandson of Ephraim Sawyer, Lieutenant-Colonel Continental Army;
> *Also*, Grandson of James Sawyer, Ensign Continental Army.

SCOVILLE, JOHN JAY. San Francisco.

> Great-grandson of Samuel Scoville, Jr., Ensign Connecticut Troops;
>
> *Also*, Great-great-grandson of Samuel Scoville, Sr., Private Connecticut Troops;
>
> *Also*, Great-grandson of Charles Close, Private Maryland Troops.

* SHAFTER, JAMES McMILLIAN.

> Grandson of James Shafter, Private New Hampshire Troops.

SHAFTER, COL. WILLIAM RUFUS, U. S. A. San Francisco.

> Great-grandson of James Shafter, Private New Hampshire Troops.

SHELDON, MARK. San Francisco.

> Grandson of Tilley Richardson, Jr., Captain Massachusetts Militia.

SHEPARD, ABRAHAM DUMMER. Los Angeles.

> Great-great-grandson of Nathan Dummer, Private Connecticut Militia.

SHERMAN, CHARLES HAMMOND. Alameda.

> Great-great-grandson of Hon. Daniel Sherman, Member of the Council of Safety, Woodbury, Conn.

SMEDBERG, LIEUT. WILLIAM RENWICK, JR., U. S. A. San Francisco.

> Great-great-grandson of Nathaniel Raymond, Jr., Corporal Connecticut Militia.

SMITH, CHESTER L. San Francisco.

> Great-grandson of Nathaniel Manning, Private Connecticut Militia.

SMITH, SIDNEY MASON. San Francisco.

> Great-grandson of Timothy Smith, Private New Hampshire Militia.

SMITH, TIMOTHY REED. Oakland.

> Grandson of Benjamin Smith, Private Massachusetts Troops.

43

SPENCER, GEORGE WILLIG. San Francisco.
>Great-grandson of Daniel Starr, Lieutenant U. S. Frigate *Trumbull*.

STAFFORD, WILLIAM GARDNER. San Francisco.
>Great-great-great-grandson of Abraham Whipple, Commodore United States Navy.

STARK, JOHN FRANCIS. Oakland.
>Great-grandson of John Stark, Brevet Major-General Continental Army.

STEARNS, ROBERT SWARTOUT. San Diego.
>Great-great-grandson of John Hays, Major Virginia Militia.

ST. JOHN, CHAUNCEY MILTON. San Francisco.
>Great great-grandson of Matthias St. John, Corporal Connecticut Militia.

STURGES, FRANKLIN FANNING. San Francisco.
>Great-grandson of Charles Fanning, Lieutenant Connecticut Troops.

SUMNER, CAPTAIN CHARLES A. San Francisco.
>Great-grandson of Hezekiah Sumner, Lieutenant Massachusetts Troops.

SUMNER, COLONEL FRANK WILLIAM. San Francisco.
>Great-grandson of William Sumner;
Also, Great-great-grandson of John Sumner, Privates Massachusetts Troops.

TALIAFERRO, BENJAMIN WATKINS. San Francisco.
>Great-grandson of Benjamin Taliaferro, Colonel Continental Army, Virginia Line.

*TAYLOR, CAPTAIN AUGUSTINE C.
>Son of James Taylor, Private Continental Army, Massachusetts Line.

TERRY, WALLACE IRVING, M. D. San Francisco.

> Great-great-grandson of William Mott, Captain New York Militia.

TOWNE, ARTHUR GOWING. San Francisco.

> Great-great-grandson of Joshua Harden, Lieutenant Massachusetts Militia.

TOWNSEND, EUGENE DeKAY. San Francisco.

> Great-great-grandson of Kilian Van Renssalaer, Colonel New York Levies;
> *Also*, Great-great-grandson of William Hun, Lieutenant New York Levies;
> *Also*, Great-grandson of John de Pruyster Douw, Ensign New York Levies.

UPHAM, CHARLES CLIFTON. New York City.

> Great-grandson of Joseph Upham, Jr., Patriot and Member Committee of Safety.

UPHAM, ENSIGN FRANK BROOKS, U. S. N.

> Great-great-grandson of Joseph Upham, Jr., Patriot and Member Committee of Safety.

UPHAM, CAPTAIN FRANK KIDDER, U. S. A. Santa Monica.

> Great-grandson of Joseph Upham, Jr., Patriot and Member Committee of Safety.

UPHAM, ISAAC. San Francisco.

> Great-grandson of Jabez Upham, Sergeant Massachusetts Militia.

VANDERCOOK, EDWARD PICKETT. Oakland.

> Great-grandson of Simon Vandercook, Ensign New York Militia.

VANDERCOOK, ROBERTS. San Francisco.

> Grandson of Simon Vandercook, Ensign New York Militia.

VARNUM, GEORGE WASHINGTON. Los Angeles.

> Grandson of Joseph Bradley Varnum, Captain Massachusetts Militia.

The People of the State of New York

By the Grace of God: FREE and INDEPENDENT.

To Simon Van Derbeck Gent. Greeting

WE reposing especial Trust and Confidence, as well in your Patriotism, Conduct and Loyalty, as in your Valour and Readiness to do us good and faithful Service, _____

_____ Have appointed and constituted, and by these Presents do appoint and constitute you the said Simon Van Derbeck Ensign of a _____ Company ___ whereof _____ Van Derbeck is intended _____

YOU are therefore, to take the said Company _____ into your charge and care as Ensign _____ thereof _____ and duly to exercise the Officers and Soldiers of that Company in Arms, who are hereby commanded to obey you as their Ensign _____ and you are also to observe and follow such Orders and Directions as you shall from time to time receive from our General and Commander in chief of the Militia of our said State, or any other your superior Officer according to the Rules and discipline of War in pursuance of the Trust reposed in you, and for so doing This shall be Your Commission, for and during our good pleasure, to be signified by our Council of Appointment. In Testimony whereof we have caused our Seal for Military Commissions to be hereunto affixed. Witness our Trusty and well beloved George Clinton ___ our Governor of our said _____ General and Commander in chief of all the Militia and Admiral of the Navy of the same, by and with the advice and consent of our said Council of Appointment, at _____ the _____ day of _____ in the _____ year of our Independence, and in the year of our Lord, one Thousand seven Hundred and seventy eight

Passed the Secretary's Office. _____ 17 __

By His Excellency's Command

VREELAND, EZEKIEL BISHOP. San Francisco.
Grandson of Abraham Vreeland, Private New Jersey Troops.

WAGENER, SAMUEL HOPKINS. San Jose.
Great-grandson of Amos Cutting West, Private Connecticut
Militia.

WALLACE, CHARLES DETTIMAS. Fitchburg.
Great-grandson of Uriah Wallace, Lieutenant New York
Levies.

* WALLACE, COLONEL URIAH.
Grandson of Uriah Wallace, Colonel New York Levies.

WALTON, MARTIN CLINTON. San Francisco.
Great-grandson of Dr. John Young, Surgeon Continental
Army, New York Line.

WARD, JOSEPH WALTER. Oakland.
Great-great-grandson of Artemas Ward, Major-General Continental Army.

WARFIELD, GENERAL RICHARD HENRY. San Francisco.
Great-grandson of Whitney Hill, Sergeant Massachusetts
Militia.

WARNER, CHARLES HUTCHINSON. San Francisco.
Great-great-great-grandson of William Talcott, Lieutenant
Connecticut Troops;
Also, Great-great-grandson of Dr. Gibbons Jewett, Surgeon Con-
necticut Troops.

WARNER, JOSIAH BUELL. San Francisco.
Great-great-great-grandson of William Talcott;
Also, Great-great-grandson of Dr. Gibbons Jewett, Surgeon Con-
necticut Troops.

WARREN, REV. JAMES HENRY, D. D. San Francisco.
Great-grandson of Abraham Warren, Private Connecticut
Militia.

WARREN, PICKETT LATIMER. Los Angeles.

Great-grandson of Asa Wheelock, Private Massachusetts Troops;

Also, Great-great-grandson of Nathaniel Warren;

Also, Great-grandson of Stephen Warren;

Also, Great-great-grandson of Ebenezer Read, Privates Massachusetts Militia.

WASHINGTON, FRANKLIN BEDINGER. San Francisco.

Great-great-grandson of Samuel Washington, Colonel;

Also, Great-grandson of Thornton Washington, Ensign Virginia Militia.

WATERMAN, AUGUSTUS. San Francisco.

Great-great-grandson of Rev. James Sproat, D. D., Chaplain Pennsylvania Troops;

Also, Great-grandson of Joseph Spencer, Lieutenant Pennsylvania Militia.

* WHIPPLE, CAPTAIN STEPHEN G., U. S. A.

Grandson of Jonathan Whipple, Private Massachusetts Militia.

WHITNEY, JAMES ORLANDO. San Francisco.

Great-grandson of Samuel Senter, Private New Hampshire Militia.

* WILDER, COLONEL DAVID.

Great-grandson of David Wilder, Major Massachusetts Troops.

* WILLIAMS, BENJAMIN FRANKLIN.

Grandson of Thomas Williams, Sergeant Connecticut Militia.

WILLIAMS, FRANK. San Francisco.

Great-grandson of James Williams, Jr., Major Massachusetts Militia.

WILLIAMS, FRANKLIN DELAMORE. San Francisco.

Great-grandson of Thomas Williams, Sergeant Connecticut Militia.

WILLIAMS, GEORGE NELSON. San Francisco.
> Grandson of Timothy Olmstead, Musician Connecticut Militia.

* WINTER, WILLIAM.
> Grandson of John Winter, Ensign New Jersey Troops.

WITHINGTON, DAVID LITTLE. San Diego.
> Great-great-great-grandson of Moses Little, Colonel Continental Army, Massachusetts Line.

---

* Deceased.

Instructions to Applicants.

The application must be presented in duplicate upon the form issued by the National Society.

The record of the ancestors' service should be given fully but concisely.

It is not necessary to show the pedigree any further back than the ancestor who served in the war.

The Society does not accept *Encyclopedias, Genealogical Works, or Town or County Histories*, except such as contain *Rosters* as authorities for proofs of service.

In referring to printed books the volume and page should be given.

Reference to authorities, in manuscript, must be accompanied by certified copies, and authentic family records submitted, if required.

Every application must be accompanied by Ten Dollars ($10.00), signed and sworn by the applicant and endorsed by two members of the Society.

When the applicant is not personally known to any member of the Society whom he can ask to recommend his application, he must submit to the Secretary, when he files his papers, the names of two reputable citizens of the State, to whom he refers by permission.

When an applicant claims descent from more than one Revolutionary ancestor, then "Supplementary" applications must be made in duplicate for each ancestor.

Supplementary claims are to be treated in form and procedure precisely as original applications. No extra cost for filing supplementary claims.

Roll of Honor.

	Page
Abbott, Capt. Joshua	22
Abbott, Lieut. Josiah	30
Allen, Jacob	40
Anderson, Capt. James	28
Anderson, Col. Richard Clough	22
Andros, Rev. Thomas	22
Austin, Levi	22
Ayer, William	23
Bailey, Major Asa	23
Bailey, Capt. Paul	23
Baker, Jeremiah	32
Bancroft, Aaron	28
Barker, Timothy	23
Barton, Col. William	28
Bartlett, Lieut. Stephen	23
Bellows, Lieut. Col. Joseph	23
Berry, John	24
Blake, Lieut. John	24, 25
Boardman, Oliver	24
Bonnell, Aaron	24
Booth, Sergeant Walter	24
Bradley, Col. Phillip Burr	35
Brandegee, Elishaman	24
Bromley, William	24, 25
Brooks, Lieut. Almarin, Sr	39
Burbeck, Capt. Edward	25
Burbeck, Col. William	25
Burnett, Sergeant James	25
Burnham, Capt. James	25
Burnham, Seth	25
Burt, Lieut. David	26
Burton, Elizah	26
Butler, Col. Zebulon	26
Byram, Ebenezer	32

	Page
Cady, Eleazar	34
Carleton, Lieut. Jeremiah	33
Carpenter, Benjamin	38
Carter, Capt. John	38
Casey, Wanton	30
Catlin, Lieut. David	26
Childs, Aaron	30
Clark, Lieut. Isaac	33, 34
Clark, Capt. Stephen	26
Cleveland, Solomon	25
Cleveland, Sergeant Stephen	26
Close, Charles	42
Cogswell, Surgeon William	26
Cook, Jr., Lieut. Col. Isaac	27
Corliss, Joshua	27
Crary, John	27
Cresap, Lieut. Daniel, Jr	33, 39
Crosby, Capt. Josiah	36
Currier, Sergeant David	27
Cutler, Thomas	27
Outter, Ammi	27
Cutter, Lieut. Samuel	27
Cutting, Sergeant Jonas	27
Daggett, Rev. Naphthali	28
Danforth, Corporal William	28
Davidson, Thomas	36
Davis, Lieut. Isaac	28
Dayton, Capt. John	28
DeBow, Capt. John	37
DeMier, Capt. John	35
Dewey, Rev. Jedediah	39
Dimock, Sergeant Timothy	35
Dimon, Ensign Daniel	28
Douw, Ensign John de Pruyster	44
DuBois, Peter	29
Dummer, Nathan	42
Dutton, Samuel	29
Eastin, Sergeant William	29

Page

Ellery, William, Signer 26
Everts, Sergeant Ambrose..................................... 29
Fairfield, William 39
Fanning, Lieut. Charles.. 43
Fanning, Walter 22
Farrar, Humphrey.. 38
Farrar, Capt. Samuel 38
Farrington, Josiah... 29
Faulkner, William 32
Fernald, Hercules Archelaus 29
Finch, Lieut. John 29
Flint, Surgeon Thomas 29
Folsom, Benjamin 29
Folson, Lieut. Jonathan 29
Franklin, Benjamin... 23
Frisbey, William 36
Frost, General John 26
Gates, Capt. Isaac 38
George, Jesse.. 30
Goodale, Major Nathan.. 30
Goodridge, Daniel 22
Graves, Josiah... 26
Gray, Isaiah... 30
Gray, John.. 30
Green, Abiathar 30
Green, Thomas... 30
Greenawalt, Philip Lorenz..................................... 30
Greene, Commander Christopher 30
Gunsaul, John... 36
Hale, Dr. William 31
Hall, Sergeant Moses 23
Hall, Timothy... 31
Halstead, Joseph 31
Hancock, Corporal Allen...................................... 35
Harden, Lieut. Joshua.. 44
Harkness, Lieut. John 32
Harrison, Benjamin, Signer 14
Hawley, Sergeant Thomas 32

4

	Page
Hays, Major John	43
Hazlet, Andrew	31
Head, Capt. Nathaniel	32
Hichborn, Lieut. Robert	31
Hill, Sergeant Whitney	45
Holden, Capt. Samuel	33
Hollnday, Samuel	33
Hollister, David	36
Holt, Valentine	34
Hooker, Seth	25
Hooper, George	33
Houghton, Capt. Benjamin	33
Hubbard, Ensign Peter, Jr	33, 34
Hubbell, Corporal Abijah	34
Hubbell, Gershom	34
Hun, Lieut. William	44
Hunt, Col. Thomas	34
Hunter, Col. James	34
Huntington, Sergeant James	26
Huse, Lieut. John	33
Jackson, Lieut. James	34
Jewett, Dr. Gibbons	45
Jewett, Capt. Josiah	29
Kellogg, Jason	36
Kellogg, Phineas	35
Kimball, John	35
Kimball, Capt. Reuben	35
King, Major Rufus	35
Kirby, Ensign Ephraim	24
Knox, General Henry	32
Lathrop, Jedediah, Jr	35
Lauman, Lient. Christopher	36
Leonard, Justin	23
Lewis, Abel	24
Lewis, John	36
Libbey, John	35
Little, Col. Moses	47
Livingston, Sergeant Isaac	32

5

	Page
Livingston, Robert	37
Looker, Othneil	24
Lyman, Col. Daniel	41
Manning, Nathaniel	36, 42
Mastick, Benjamin	36
Mauzy, William	36
McClintock, William	37
McHenry, Jesse	36
McKee, John	37
McKinstry, Lieut. Charles	37
McLane, Lieut. Allen	36
Meeker, Lieut. Obadiah	37
Mills, Capt. John	37
Mooers, Lieut. Benjamin	37
Moore, Lieut. Pliny	37
Morris, John	25
Mott, Capt. William	44
Moulton, General Jotham	38
Mulford, Col. David	37
Munger, Capt. James	38
Newhall, Lieut.-Col. Ezra	39
Nichols, Col. Moses	23
Nixon, Col. Thomas	40
Norcross, John	38
North, Lieut. Benjamin	38
North, Robert, Sr.	38
Norton, Peter	39
Olmstead, Timothy	47
Pack, William	39
Paddock, David	39
Page, Col. William	39
Paulding, John	37
Pelham, Major Charles	39
Perkins, Luke	28
Phelps, Eliphalet	40
Pine, Joshua	30
Platt, Capt. Nathaniel	37
Platt, Col. Zephaniah	37

Page

Plimpton, Elijah 40
Plum, John 40
Polhemus, Major John 40
Porter, Capt. Moses 32
Posey, General Thomas 40
Pratt, Capt. Josiah 40
Putnam, General Israel 26
Putman, Jacob, Jr 40
Rand, William 40
Raymond, Lieut. John 23
Raymond, Corporal Nathaniel Jr 42
Read, Ebenezer 46
Read, George, Signer 36
Read, Corporal Jacob 41
Read, Col. Seth 27
Redington, Corporal Asa 41
Reed, General James 41
Remsen, Luke 38
Requa, Abraham 41
Requa, Daniel 41
Requa, Capt. Glode 41
Rice, Lieut. Jonas 41
Richardson, Capt. John 24
Richardson, Capt. Tilley, Jr 42
Robinson, Capt. Noah 41
Root, Capt. Eli 28
Rummey, Conrad 22
Rutherford, John 41
Sargent, Winthrop 38
Sawyer, Lieut.-Col. Ephraim 41
Sawyer, Ensign James 41
Schenck, Ralph 29
Scoville, Ensign Samuel, Jr 42
Scoville, Samuel. Sr 42
Senter, Samuel 46
Shafter, James 42
Shaw, Nathaniel 38
Sherman, Hon. Daniel 42

	Page
Shields, Daniel	35
Slade, Col. Peleg	30
Slaughter, Col. James	34
Slaughter, Capt. Phillip	34
Smith, Benjamin	42
Smith, Lieut. David	34
Smith, Enoch	29
Smith, Timothy	42
Snow, Capt. Samuel	39
Spencer, Lieut. Joseph	46
Sproat, Rev. James	46
Stark, General John	43
Starr, Lieut. Daniel	43
Stedman, Simeon	27
St. John, Corporal Mathias	43
Stockwell, John	26
Sumner, Lieut. Hezekiah	43
Sumner, John	43
Sumnor, William	43
Talcott, Lieut. William	45
Taliaferro, Col. Benjamin	43
Tapley, Lieut. Gilbert	32
Tapley, Lieut. Joseph	32
Taylor, James	43
Thomas, Sergeant Malachi	34
Thorp, Capt. Eliphalet	33
Upham, Sergeant Jabez	44
Upham, Joseph, Jr	44
Upham, Samuel	28
Vandercook, Ensign Simon	44
Van Ness, Lieut. Simon	37
Van Rensselaer, Col. Kilian	34, 44
Varnum, Capt. Joseph Bradley	44
Vaughan, Surgeon Claiborne	35
Vreeland, Abraham	45
Walbridge, Silas, Sr	39
Wallace, Lieut. Uriah	45
Ward, Major-General Artemas	45

	Page
Ward, Elijah	33, 34
Ward, Gov. Samuel	30
Warren, Abraham	45
Warren, Nathaniel	46
Warren, Stephen	46
Washington, Col. Samuel	46
Washington, Ensign Thornton	46
West, Amos Cutting	45
Wheelock, Asa	46
Whipple, Commodore Abraham	43
Whipple, Jonathan	46
Whiting, Col. Daniel	32
Whiting, Lieut. Gamaliel	37
Whittemore, Capt. Samuel	27
Wilbur, John	22
Wilder, Major David	46
Wilkins, Capt. Daniel	29
Wilson, Jeremiah	33, 34
Williams, Major James, Jr	46
Williams, Sergeant Thomas	46
Winchester, Lieut. William	40
Winter, Ensign John	47
Young, Dr. John	45

ERRATA.

Page 35, read Roy Thurston Kimball.
Page 35, read Jedidiah Lathrop, Jr.
Page 37, read David Mulford.
Page 45, read Uriah Wallace, Lieutenant.